GLOW-IN-THE-DARK ADVENTURES

ALIENS

ARCTURUS

In 1996, scientists found what they thought were worm-shaped fossils on a meteorite that came from Mars.

THE GREAT UNKNOWN
You've probably learned that Earth is the only known planet to support life, but, with billions of planets in our galaxy alone, you find it hard to believe that we are alone in the universe...

Since the very first time man ventured into space, humans have been unknowingly whizzing past alien life forms. If only the astronauts could see it, far below them is a red wasteland of a planet, guarded by giant one-eyed worms and massive four-legged monsters!

PROBING THE TRUTH

Sometimes you wonder why aliens haven't responded to our messages...but that's because aliens have sent their own messages to us and their probes are currently whizzing round in space undetected. The aliens are patiently waiting for someone clever – someone like you – to discover their messages. But wait! NASA's probes carrying pictures and recordings of humans have just crashed into the distant planet Bingzangtee nearly forty years after being launched! Somewhere out there, past the swirling mists of Neptune, aliens are looking at pictures of humans, wondering what to do next...

The first human radio signals have travelled nearly a hundred light years into space – somewhere out there, aliens could be watching our 1950s TV shows!

DARK SIDE OF THE MOON

You think there's no life on the Moon because we've already been there, right? But what if you were wrong! If you had a very powerful telescope, together with the world's most powerful lens, you might be able to see the Phydadida creatures living in the Moon's craters. This is all top secret, of course, and you wouldn't be able to find it in any government files.

Fed up with human feet trampling over them and destroying their homes, the Phydadidans have had enough! The humans had better watch out, because they've decided it's finally time to visit Earth…

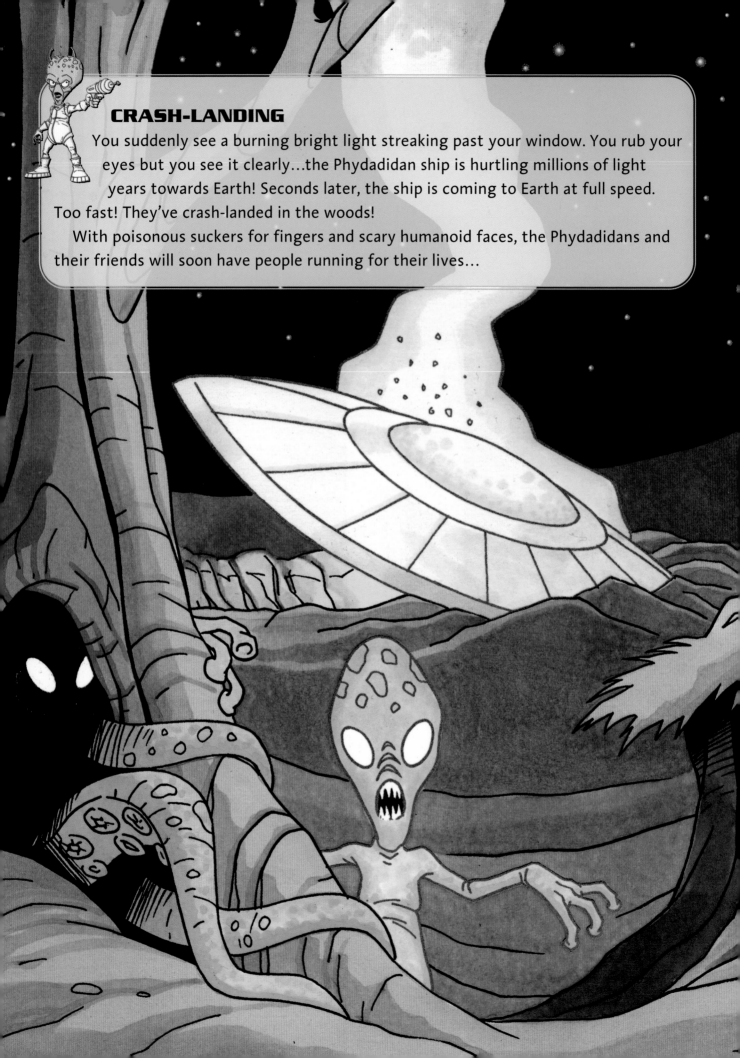

CRASH-LANDING

You suddenly see a burning bright light streaking past your window. You rub your eyes but you see it clearly...the Phydadidan ship is hurtling millions of light years towards Earth! Seconds later, the ship is coming to Earth at full speed. Too fast! They've crash-landed in the woods!

With poisonous suckers for fingers and scary humanoid faces, the Phydadidans and their friends will soon have people running for their lives...

Worldwide, there are 70,000 reported UFO (Unidentified Flying Object) sightings every year. That means an average of 192 per day!

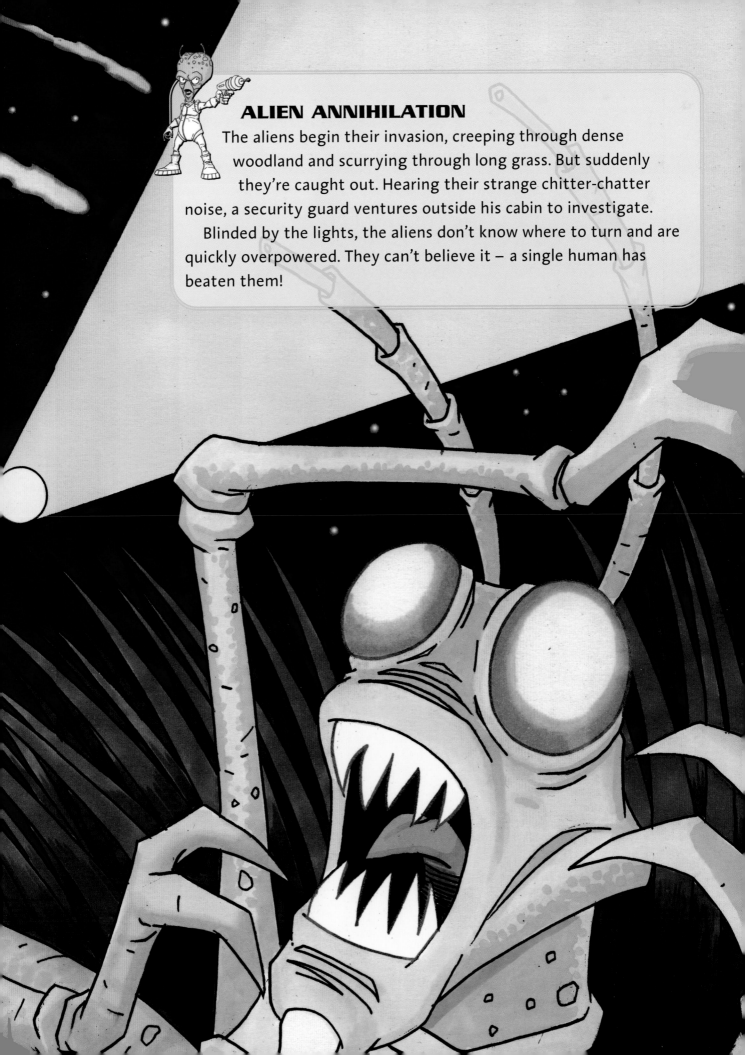

ALIEN ANNIHILATION

The aliens begin their invasion, creeping through dense woodland and scurrying through long grass. But suddenly they're caught out. Hearing their strange chitter-chatter noise, a security guard ventures outside his cabin to investigate. Blinded by the lights, the aliens don't know where to turn and are quickly overpowered. They can't believe it – a single human has beaten them!

REVENGE OF THE ZEONIANS

In a galaxy far away, aliens from the planet Zeon have been watching the Phydadidans' failed attack on Earth. Furious with the humans at their treatment of their fellow aliens, they decide to launch their own attack. Within just hours, they fly past the rings of Saturn and up over the Moon, landing at Roswell, USA.

The Zeonians plan to destroy all human life using their infrared nanotron laser guns! People flee from their homes, terrified. Around the world, governments are working on a plan to fight back.

Welcome to
ROSWELL

357

In 1947 in Roswell, New Mexico, USA, an alien spaceship supposedly crashed and experiments were conducted on a dead alien's body.

There are more UFO sightings in the USA than in the UK, with around 300 reported sightings a year.

BACK TO REALITY

The alien threat has lasted for three days and panic is widespread. Early one evening, the radio crackles sharply and announces that the Zeonians have been beaten!

In the distance, you hear a low buzzing, which is getting closer and louder. You join the rest of the neighbourhood and look up, watching as the Zeonians leave. You feel overwhelmed with joy, relieved and excited at the same time. But somewhere deep down, you wonder if perhaps it wouldn't be so bad if they'd stayed after all…

ALIENS:
THE FACTS

In 1964, New Mexico, USA, a policeman claimed to have scared off some aliens who had crashed their spaceship. Police found burning grass and scorched, rocket-blasted ground.

We are still waiting for a reply to a radio message broadcast to the distant star cluster M13 in 1974. An alien response would take 48,000 years to reach Earth.

Scientists believe that there may be an ocean on one of Jupiter's moons containing undiscovered life forms.

Astronaut Scott Carpenter reportedly photographed a UFO while in orbit on 24 May, 1962.

ARCTURUS

This edition published in 2008 by
Arcturus Publishing Limited
26/27 Bickels Yard, 151–153 Bermondsey Street,
London SE1 3HA

Copyright © 2008 Arcturus Publishing Limited

All rights reserved. No part of this publication may be reproduced, stored in a retrieval system, or transmitted, in any form or by any means, electronic, mechanical, photocopying, recording or otherwise, without written permission in accordance with the provisions of the Copyright Act 1956 (as amended). Any person or persons who do any unauthorised act in relation to this publication may be liable to criminal prosecution and civil claims for damages.

ISBN: 978-1-84193-921-6

Printed in China

Authors: Fiona Tulloch and Ben Hubbard
Illustrator: Steve Beaumont
Editor: Fiona Tulloch
Designer: Steve Flight